How to Move on
after a Divorce

*An Essential Guide
to Coping with Divorce,
Moving on, and Creating
a Happy New Life*

by Janelle Novak

Table of Contents

Introduction

The papers have been signed and the divorce is final. You are faced with the grim reality that things will never be the same again. You knew this was coming; you were there for the proceedings after all. And yet this finality somehow still comes as a shock. You know that you need to move on but cannot lift a finger to go forward. You know that you need to initiate drastic changes in your life immediately. Yet you just stare at the empty spaces once occupied by your ex-partner. You now find yourself clutching this book and desperately seeking answers.

Do you want to stop feeling like your world has come to an end? Do you want to feel less exhausted — physically and emotionally? Do you want to get up from your bed and shake off the feeling that you just want to sleep and never wake up? Do you want to see your old happy and energetic self instead of that sullen stranger staring at you in the mirror? Do you want to remember how it is to feel love and happiness again?

If your answer is yes to any (or all) of the above questions, then you were right in picking this book. Be forewarned though, this book will not serve as a magic wand with which you can make all your troubles vanish. This book will also not guarantee that you will find love and get married again in the next few days or even in the next few years.

I'm going to help steer you in the right direction, onto a new path with simple but concrete steps to find yourself and your sense of passion again. I'm going to help you reignite your positive energy and ward off all the pain and drama you had to deal with during your divorce. You will gain confidence to achieve a new, healthier and happier version of yourself even after all that you have been through. This book will serve as a simple but practical and effective guide to heal yourself. So take a deep breath, hold your head high and take heart in the knowledge that you can turn your life around whenever you are ready to. If you decide that moment is now, then let's get started!

Chapter 1: Celebrating Your New Life

Be grateful for your new lease on life.

The papers may have been signed and the divorce final, but it is not the end of the world. The end of your marriage does not mean that your life will come to a standstill. When one journey ends, yet another begins. Wherever you are and whatever your background and status in life, simply embrace the changes you now face and move on with grace and gratitude. Be grateful that you still have the chance to rectify past mistakes and create a new life for yourself. Everything may seem hopeless and desperate right now to you. But keep calm, just take a deep breath and look forward to what the future may hold for you. Have faith that things will get better in due time.

Be happy about what you still have.

Smile even if you feel like you are going to fall down on your knees while wishing that the ground would just open up and swallow you. Smile. Smile a lot. Smile even if tears cloud your vision at the moment. Smile to cheer yourself up and those around you. The pain will soon pass. With all its sham, drudgery and broken dreams, it is still a beautiful world. An exercise that helps a lot of people, but can be hard to begin, is to start to list things you are grateful for: good health, hot coffee, the ability to see and read, the beginning of a new season. Make yourself write down things that you are thankful for as you start your day or before you go to bed at night. You can choose to list one, ten or a hundred things daily, only do as much as you want. In a few weeks you will have a long list to remind you that life isn't so bad.

Organize your life.

Begin with the most immediate and work up to the most difficult tasks. Clear out your wallet, purse/handbag or briefcase. Organize your closet. The physical, emotional and social demands on your life at the moment have led you to a tailspin and the feeling of sinking into quicksand, all at once. Thus, it is important to maintain a semblance of order, beginning with the most obvious aspects of your life such as your immediate surroundings. Put the remaining possessions of your ex-spouse in storage. Clear all old messages from your phone as well as your email.

Let go of the past.

Get out of bed. If you have been wallowing in self-pity and could not get out bed for days or even weeks, get up immediately. Take a cold, refreshing shower or a long leisurely warm bath. Clean every part of your body as if you were willing all the bad energy to wash off you and go down the drain. The shower or bath should leave you feeling a little less depressed and more upbeat about the future. These small steps will occupy your troubled mind and allow you to move forward, slowly but surely, toward freedom from past hurts and emotional baggage.

Let go of the past and face your future with courage. Wash away any physical reminder of your pain and all remnants of your sad past. Begin by putting all the soiled clothes from your hamper in the washer. Mop or vacuum your bedroom, the living room and the rest of your home. Change the linen and clean your entire bedroom. Work steadily, even doggedly, to clear any old baggage from the past to make way for your new life. This will make it easier for you to face your new life, to start over with a clean slate.

Chapter 2: Finding Strength, Inside and Out

Know and understand yourself.

Another crucial step to turning your life around after divorce is to find and rediscover yourself. In order to find a new purpose and a new path in life, you must gain a clear understanding of yourself as a person. Grab some colorful pens and a large clean illustration board. Make two columns in your board, mark the first one "present" and the other "future". In the "present", write down your present situation, traits and characteristics. Think of areas that you wish to change or improve about yourself. Start with the most obvious ones like the fact that you need to lose those extra thirty pounds you put on during pregnancy or from heavy drinking and binge eating. In the "future", write down all the things you want to change about yourself. Include in the second column your new goals and dreams.

Nurture yourself and your loved ones.

Head to your kitchen. Wash all the used utensils, dirty pans and filthy dishes that have piled up in the sink.

Clean your pantry and fridge. Throw away everything expired and maybe the unhealthy junk food. Go food-shopping for healthy, organically grown and nutritious food. Start cooking healthy and delicious meals for yourself and for your family, especially if you have young children. You and your family need to keep going despite the havoc wrought by the divorce on your family life. Shower your family with love and affection.

Get to work.

Clear and organize your work desk at home and at the office. Organize your mail and email inbox. Sort all your files. If you were a stay-at-home parent when you were married and are now faced with having to support yourself and your children, explore your options. Ask for help from your circle of friends and family. The divorce may have disrupted and turned your life upside down, but you now have the chance to get back on your feet, to be financially free and independent.

Be financially free.

Being divorced now allows you the financial freedom and independence you may not have enjoyed when you were still married. For instance, you do not need to pay for expenses that your spouse racked up on credit, such as those expensive dresses or that extra set of golf clubs, which did not contribute to the benefit of the family. Pay all your bills as soon as you can. Cut up all your credit cards when possible. Settle all the legal bills that may have accumulated over the entire divorce process. Look beyond the present and plan your financial future. Look for a new alternative career or actively seek a raise or promotion.

Care for yourself.

Care for yourself as if you were nursing a sick person back to health. That is exactly what you are from a psychological standpoint. Treat yourself as if you were caring for a sick child or your elderly parent. Loving yourself first should be top of mind now that you are trying to regain a new foothold on life.

Chapter 3: Living in Constant Grace and Goodness

Start a fitness regimen.

We all know that we need exercise to ensure good health and longevity. Find some form of exercise that you enjoy like walking, swimming or running. The best exercise for you is one which you will enjoy and will do regularly. Exercise at least five times a week for at least half an hour each day. For you in particular, you need to get out of your current difficulties and spend considerable time on getting back to shape and being fit.

If you are busy and pressed for time, break apart the exercise periods into several periods of ten or fifteen minutes each period. These shorter exercise sessions will then be easier to fit into your hectic days. Exercise will make you feel good about yourself and will make you healthier and less likely to get sick. People who exercise regularly feel healthy and are less likely to become depressed.

Do something good for others.

You can volunteer time and skills at the nearest orphanage, homeless shelter, home for the elderly or at a pet shelter. Every harvest requires an initial seed. In the same way that your family and friends were always there for you when you needed them, invest some of your energy in helping others. Do good deeds in whatever way you can give, without waiting for a reward or payment. Be generous in sowing the seeds of your goodness. On your second chance to take a hold of your life, just do whatever bit of good you can give to others. Life is too short to be wasted just wondering about what good or wonderful thing you could do. So just get on with it and just help others along the way.

Eat healthy.

Eat a variety of natural and organic foods. Include in your diet plenty of fresh fruits and vegetables. Reduce your fat intake, which should be no more than thirty percent of your total daily calorie consumption. Follow the food pyramid and stick to a varied diet that is low in fat and cholesterol but high in fiber. A healthy diet can help lower your risk of cancer and other life threatening illnesses. Always eat healthy and set a good example for your kids. Choose fresh fruit and vegetables that are in season. Good nutrition should start at an early age and not when you are already sick or obese.

Breathe deeply and meditate.

Making a habit of breathing deeply helps reduce tension and stress. Deep breathing also helps you keep your lungs working properly and efficiently. Whenever you begin to feel tense, breathe slowly and deeply for a few minutes.

Give love and affection freely.

You may have been burned and hurt deeply by the way your marriage ended but that is no excuse to shut out the world. There are people—family and friends—who are ready to help you if you just reach out. It may still be hard to be a fountain of affection because of how you were treated by your ex-spouse. Love your children, the rest of your family and your friends unguardedly and unconditionally even if you are still hurting. If we want to feel loved once more, we must start giving love freely and unconditionally. Soon all that love will flow back to you.

Chapter 4: Raising Yourself and Carrying Your Burden Well

Take a step at a time.

There will be days when you will still feel that your whole world is crumbling down. Instead of allowing yourself to get sucked back into all that negativity again, just put one foot in front of the other and keep going. Each time you feel like you are about to fall, catch yourself and raise yourself up. Cherish the small joys of being alive. Check your emails and reply positively to each one. Go to your meetings, get to work and attend to your business. It's the little things that buoy you up and get you through the big upheavals such as your divorce.

Deal with stress constructively.

The changes you are going through right now are stressful, to say the least. You just went through a divorce and are likely to be facing other major changes as a result of it, you might have to move from your home or to another location. The stress of the divorce and the many changes that come after, also lead to many behavioral and emotional problems such as anxiety and depression. Do not let these stresses accumulate and make you physically ill.

Ask for support when you need it.

At this point in time, you may feel at your most vulnerable. Ask for strength to overcome your current difficulties and you will receive it. Do the same with your family and friends. When you feel like you are unable to go on, call your parents, your best friend or your siblings. If you are having problems and cannot deal with it alone, call someone who can help, your best friend or a close relative. Help will always come to those who know how to ask for it, especially in the most critical moments.

Pray and keep the faith.

It does not matter what faith or religion you subscribe to, just remember to hold on to faith and to pray. Pause for a moment and lift your cares and troubles to God and pray for help. Even for those who profess a different faith, you may elevate all your cares to a higher power. Trusting that someone else will help you carry your burden will ease the load you carry. Pray constantly. It is the moments when we feel most alone when we are with God or a divine and higher being than ourselves. Recognize that you need faith and to trust fully at this point. When all else fails, keep calm and pray for help.

Spend time with family and friends.

Have breakfast with your kids before you go to work. Have lunch with your friends. Go for a run with your buddies. Take your dog for a long walk in the park. Invite your parents and siblings over for a home-cooked dinner. Kids spell love as time. The same goes for your family and friends. The little everyday moments count. Play with your toddler. Bring your family to the beach or for a weekend island getaway. Go shopping with your children. Run errands with your parents or siblings. You don't have to have big vacation plans to relax and spend time with them. Even just hanging out at home with family, having a barbecue, is a special and wonderful treat for them and for yourself.

Chapter 5: Charting Your New Path

Make an action plan.

Now that you have written down what you want to achieve at present and in the long-term future, choose three of the most immediate goals. The top three goals you choose must be attainable within the next few hours, days, weeks and months. Make a to-do list of what you will do to attain those top three goals. Let's say you want to lose around twenty pounds. Make a list of five things you will do that will ensure that you will shed those excess pounds within the next three to six months. An example of to-do's for this goal would include getting rid of all fattening food from your pantry and fridge as well as exercising for at least an hour every day. Do the same for the rest of your immediate goals and discipline yourself to stick with these to-do's within the time you indicated in your action plan.

Stay fit.

Stick to your chosen fitness regimen to keep your body trim. You need exercise not only for physical fitness but also for mental and psychological balance. Choose the right fitness plan for you that will not hamper your new lifestyle and schedule.

If you are overweight, make definite changes in your eating and exercise habits. Do not let yourself or your children become overweight. Remember that obesity is directly linked with many serious diseases such as heart ailment and diabetes. Leading a healthy lifestyle for you and your family is one of the most important things you can do for yourself at this point in your life.

Get a makeover.

Change your hairstyle or your entire look. Allotting even five minutes to put on makeup can make a big difference in your confidence. Allow yourself some luxury like a new dress or even a whole new wardrobe, especially after you successfully shed all those excess pounds. That new suit or a new pair of shoes would do you a world of good and totally boost your confidence. It is part of caring for yourself and investing in yourself and in your new life. You are your own treasure and best resource. So pamper yourself. Go ahead, redefine and reinvent yourself.

Get rid of bad habits.

If you smoke or drink, quit now. Smoking not only causes heart disease, it also accelerates the aging of your skin, bones and lungs. Smoking also causes lung cancer and is a major contributory factor in developing cancers of the esophagus, mouth, throat, bladder and cervix. If you drink alcohol, do so only occasionally and in great moderation. If you have a problem with alcohol or substance abuse, call your physician or seek professional help. Now that you are turning over a new leaf, it is the best time to chuck those old habits.

Get a good night's sleep.

Lack of sleep is generally harmless unless you become overtired or too tense because of it. Chronic insomnia is usually a symptom of deeper problems such as anxiety and depression. If lack of sleep affects your daily routine, consult your doctor.

Chapter 6: Living Simply but Fully

Keep a positive outlook.

Do not allow yourself to be overcome by stress and become increasingly susceptible to physical or mental illness, behavioral and emotional problems and even injuries. Even if the tremendous amount of stress you are going through does not cause mental or physical illness, you and your family are likely to be adversely affected. Deal with the stress positively by addressing what is important and immediate. As much as possible, do not allow it to negatively impact your quality of life. The divorce has already caused enough upheaval, so do not permit a domino-like effect on your life and those of your kids and loved ones.

Laugh your worries away.

Use humor to take the edge off the pain. Perhaps at first you let yourself laugh out loud not fully enjoying the joke. But the moment you let yourself go and enjoy the humor, you will instantly feel your tense muscles relax. So laugh your heart out. Laughter produces an intense release of energy in a short span of time. It even lets you lose weight—one minute of laughter burns 1.3 calories. Laughter oxygenates body cells and clears air passages. A burst of laughter massages internal organs and lowers cortisol or stress hormones. More importantly, laughter releases endorphins or feel-good hormones and helps you fight depression. Laughter is indeed medicine.

Energize your spirit.

We all cope with stress and failure differently. We also all have various sources of emotional stress. At this point in time, you are most vulnerable and most likely to suffer from depression. Learn to recognize the symptoms immediately. There are different degrees of depression. Some tend to be temporarily demoralized but soon get back on their feet. Others get anxiety attacks. In worse case scenarios, some people become extremely depressed and suicidal. Should you need professional help, do so immediately.

See your doctor.

Go to regular medical checkups. Get screened for all types of possible illnesses especially the ones which run in your family. Get psychiatric help if you have the symptoms of clinical depression like chronic insomnia and intense anxiety. Screening tests can detect many diseases and catch them at the early stages when it can still be successfully treated.

Avoid chaos and negativity.

This is easier said than done. Go placidly amid the noise, bustle and worry. Find silence. Find solitude. Find peace. Be on good terms as much as possible with the people around you. Some bridges may be burning but it is best to repair what is left and build new ones around you. Listen to others. Avoid loud and aggressive persons so that your spirit will be spared from further vexation. Try not to be bitter and cynical despite what you are going through. Do not further distress yourself with worry and fear and loneliness.

Chapter 7: Rewriting Your Story

Be present in the moment.

Follow your action plan and commit to achieving those goals. Embrace each moment with gratitude and love. It is not a world catastrophe that your marriage has ended. What would be a disaster is when you give up and just let your hopes and dreams fade away unfulfilled. While there is life still left in you, do not give up longing and wishing for your dreams to come true. Each moment is a precious gift that should not be wasted pining for what is past and gone. Find all that is beautiful and good. Find the positive energy inside you and channel these to attain your goals and dreams. It does not matter if you are newly single and alone now, just live and love! Be happy and complete in yourself and nothing else matters.

Always strive to find balance in the little moments.

Take delight in a good book, your children's sweet smiles and doodles on the fridge door. Dealing with the stress and all the emotions that come with a divorce should just be part of your balancing act. Do not give up any of your dreams just because one dream ended badly. Certainly, the many difficulties you currently face are quite overwhelming but you can always take a deep breath and look at things calmly and differently. Everything will eventually fall into place. Down the road, you may even learn to be friends with your ex-partner once more, especially if you need to raise your young kids despite your new status and new arrangements.

Be both the seeker and the doer in your new life.

Be a witness to your own life as it unfolds and slowly transforms you into the stronger and better person that this phase is honing you to be. The divorce and the many difficulties that you are going through are simply a means to transform you into the better person you are becoming, one blessed day at a time. Just remember that everything happens for a reason. Perhaps your marriage ended because something better is in store for you—a greater love or the fulfillment of your biggest goals in life. Just take the reins of your new life firmly in your hands and steer it into a new and positive direction. Be constantly thankful for each day and all the blessings that come with it.

Rewrite your story.

Here you are with the rare chance to change the course of the rest of your new life. Do not squander this wonderful opportunity. The ending to that part of your previous life may not have gone as you thought it would. The fairy tale ending to your marriage may have fallen through but you have the great opportunity to rewrite a new and happy ending to the rest of your life. Look at life from a new perspective now that you have let go of all the negative aspects from your marriage. Find love and happiness in the littlest and simplest of things. It may sound hollow or unrealistic right now to say that you will overcome what you are going through. But you will soon come to a point when you can look back and say that you went through that dark and difficult part of your life and survived.

Conclusion

Stay with those who really matter.

You have your whole life ahead of you. You are free to spend all that time loving yourself and those around you. Interact with the world around you as you strive to embrace the changes you now have to deal with. Give love and hope in small ways to those around you. Your life is a gift best spent with those you love and who love you right back. Share your life and your love with your family and friends. It may seem very hard right now to be a fountain of love given how you are still hurting after the divorce. Living and loving takes a great deal of time and effort especially when you are going through a very rough patch.

Engage yourself in a constant flow of love and positivity.

When it comes to your life and your career, don't plan too far ahead. Just keep moving forward in a new and positive direction until you realize your full potential. Your biggest goals and dreams can be attained with the small steps you take each single day. Instead of moping and pining for what could have been, be prepared instead to embrace the many changes that you are facing now. Come to terms with the fact that things will not always happen as expected. Enjoy where you are and what you can do now. Find new love in many things, not necessarily in a new partner or a new marriage. Your love for yourself and for your family should be enough to last you the rest of your life. Do not spend the remainder of your life chasing after one failed relationship after another.

Be prepared to embrace change at every step of the way.

These are difficult times that you will be going through. The next few days, weeks, months, or even years, are all about successfully navigating the many challenges of coping with the changes that will come after the divorce. Think of the entire process as a cathartic experience, where you will exorcise all the pain and bitterness. At this point, it is crucial to face the many challenges head on while continuing to move forward in a new and positive direction.

Continue to devote a large amount of your time to improving yourself.

This is a wonderful time to learn and grow. So think of this as a cleansing process rather than letting these challenges become further obstacles to your healing and progress. Balance life's many stresses and constant pressures. Just relentlessly embrace each challenge that comes. Be grateful for the gift of each day. Take heart and face everything with love and courage. Soon enough, you will get there. If you go somewhere you don't feel comfortable in, you'll learn a lot about yourself and it will help you grow.

Do not worry too much.

If you are constantly plagued with difficult questions, just take a deep breath and think positive thoughts. Worrying about what the future holds for you now that the divorce is final will just bring you several steps backward. You are neither the first nor the last person to grapple with questions like these.

Many successful people have failed many times before but picked themselves up and raised themselves to the success stories they are now. The same holds true for those whose marriages didn't work out and eventually got divorced.

Again, remember to feel happy and complete on your own. When a journey ends, another one begins. When a door closes, a window or a new door opens. People come and go in our lives. Even our own children eventually leave the family home to start their own families and pursue their own dreams.

Many people have been on the same path before you and have survived divorce. Rise to the challenge and prove your own mettle. You are your own master now and the author of the story that is the rest of your life. Rewrite your life into the happy ending you want it to have. Write the tale of how you survived divorce and escaped the cycle of despair you are currently stuck in.

Living and loving is a process, a life-long one. Even as you are focused on dealing with the immediate needs such as juggling work and parenting, possibly making ends meet, try to keep your focus on the higher goals you have set for yourself in the new life that you are charting. There is always hope even when the present reality is so grim and dark. Just keep on loving those who matter and you will find that the circumstances will soon change for the better.

As you live, love and transform yourself from the mess you are right now, continually seek your purpose and direction. Beyond meeting your material and physical needs, learn to devote yourself to the higher purpose you have been assigned.

Some philosopher once said that the only certain thing in life is change and we fully agree. The best we can do is make sure that with the changes that come our way, we take away the valuable lessons that come with each life event and do our best not to forget. While change is the only constant in life, we can also make sure that the lessons and the growth and transformation that comes with the changes are also certain.

Even if you feel that the present challenges you are facing go beyond your capacity to cope and survive, just keep pushing on, putting one foot in front of the other until you have reached your proverbial Everest, the peak of which signifies your recovery from the divorce.

In time you will look back and just ask yourself that you don't know for sure how you survived the divorce and its aftermath but all that matters is that you did. Sooner or later, this dark time in your life will just be a distant memory.

Finally, I'd like to thank you for purchasing this book! If you found it helpful, I'd greatly appreciate it if you'd take a moment to leave a review on Amazon. Thank you!

83157593R00026

Made in the USA
Columbia, SC
09 December 2017